D1616054

LIVING LITTLE

Simplicity and style in a small space

LIVING LITTLE

Simplicity and style in a small space

images
Publishing

CONTENTS

INTRODUCTION

With living costs at an all-time high, increasing urban density, and a will to downsize and simplify our lives, the small-house typology bears prominent validity within the twenty-first century. Now recognized as a social movement, the small- or tiny-house lifestyle is underpinned by principles of financial sustainability and minimalistic living, while also being a push-back against consumer-driven societies. In addition to its social prominence, the movement has also taken reign within the architecture industry, causing much excitement. As the global population continues to rise and our cities become busier, denser, and more expensive, the sizes of our homes, too, will inevitably decrease. This reduction in the space we inhabit also means that certain things simply will not fit or have to be sacrificed. This provides architects and designers with opportunities to create innovative and precise solutions for the modern-day premium that is a space to call home. *Living Little* seeks to explore a range of small-house designs and what it means to actually be "living little." From portable hand-built trailers to tiny rooftop *casas*, to highly conceptual minimalist dwellings, the tiny-house typology presents a spectrum of space-savvy possibilities while making us question if we're indeed taking up more space than we truly need.

Although all tiny houses have one common denominator (they're significantly smaller than your average home), their purpose, and a person's decision to commence a life within one can vary significantly. One common reason, however, is the recognized value in questioning what one truly does and does not need to live. Despite being around for a while now, the concept of minimalist living seems to have merged with the small-house movement and complements it well. As tiny-house (the Matchbox) designer Jay Austin says in Netflix's well-known documentary, *Minimalism*, "We've only begun to re-examine what it means to be successful in life. It's no longer about the white picket fence or the big mansion. People are beginning to recognize that maybe they have been tricked and that maybe they have more agency over their options than they once thought they did."

Ideas such as these put under review the status quo and make us question whether preconceived notions about the types of dwelling we aspire to have, not to mention the number of objects within them, are really in our best interests.

Two others big on small footprints and living with less are Chris and Cameron Grant. After making a very deliberate leap beyond the mainstream, they founded Unyoked and made it their mission to remedy the over-stimulation of everyday Western life. How? By encouraging holidaymakers to be content with less while escaping urban density to spend uninterrupted time in nature. The result is a network of tiny, architecturally designed holiday cabins tucked away in the Australian wilderness. Another great example of living little intentionally is TACO's Casa de Monte. Immersed in the wild landscape of southeastern Mexico, it offers a very simple but functional living experience that dissipates modern-day distractions while enabling reflection and contemplation.

The small-house typology aligns well with today's demands also because it provides a potential solution to ever-increasing population growth. Urban density and housing availability are fast becoming a worldwide issue. According to the United Nations' *World Urbanization Prospects Report 2018*, by 2030, 60 percent of the world's population will reside in urban areas. These alarming statistics were only recently revealed, but architects have been trying to reinvent how humankind inhabits urban environments for years now. Moshe Safdie's Habitat 67 was completed in 1967 and intended to open minds to the possibilities of high-density living. Described as "a three-dimensional building system," it (for its time) encapsulated innovative ideas about prefabrication and reinventing apartment design. Other similar and more contemporary ideas are presented throughout this book, such as El Sindicato Arquitectura's Casa Parasito. This project seeks to solve basic habitation needs and positively contribute to the densification of a city by making use of underused, but structurally sound spaces like rooftops. Tsai Design's

Type Street Apartment is also a good example of making use of existing space. Once an average, one-bedroom apartment, it has been completely re-purposed into a highly functional and seemingly spacious dwelling. This was achieved through the architects' remarkable design intuition—knowing where it pays to be generous, using every last inch of space to their advantage.

This book demonstrates that while downsizing and jumping on the micro-living bandwagon (whatever the purpose) might mean a reduction in the size of our homes, it most certainly does not mean we have to compromise on design and the quality of life. And we can also still make positive contributions to wider issues like the environment. The projects presented in *Living Little* are proof that architects and designers can impressively rise to the occasion when faced with spatial challenges. In doing so, they pave a new way of living, create beautiful, tiny homes, and play a pivotal role in the future of housing on a global scale.

Hannah Jenkins is the editor and writer of several high-profile compilation titles on global contemporary residential architecture.

A GREAT SMALL APARTMENT

Tel Aviv, Israel
388 ft² (36 m²)
Design: Nitzan Horovitz
Photography: Oded Smadar

Located in an old building in Florentine, Tel Aviv, the interior design of this once problematic space has been transformed into a compact, but highly functional apartment. Due to its tricky dimensions and unusual division of floors (one is half a meter above street level and the other is almost two meters below), the redesign required structural amendments, which meant removing interior walls and replacing a supporting column with a beam.

From the entrance landing, two staircases diverge: one leading to the basement where the bedroom and bathing area are located, and the second rising into the gallery floor where there is a living room, a kitchen with a dining table, and a small water closet.

Prominent design components accent the décor and add a twist of modern functionality for the residents. They include a central wall cabinet, which offers storage while serving as a tangible connection between the two floors, and the stairs, which are paved with graphite porcelain that contrast with the oak parquet floor.

Despite its size, the dwelling contains all the conveniences of a normal-size apartment, including bedside tables, washing and drying machines, a bathroom space with a sink, and a small work desk. Intended to reflect a "real" apartment as opposed to something modular or highly conceptual, the unit redefines and re-purposes old structures to create a comfortable and livable space that is simply on the smaller side.

"Intended to reflect a 'real' apartment as opposed to something modular or highly conceptual."

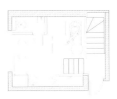

First-floor plan

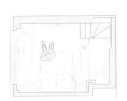

Basement-floor plan

2 4 6   9.84 ft
1 2   3 m

ARCHITECTURAL (DIS)ORDER

Quarteira, Portugal
323 ft² (30 m²)
Design: Corpo Atelier
Photography: Alexander Bogorodskiy

Inside a white box, three differently configured yellow objects have been individually placed. The idea behind this abstract design concept was to challenge, and dramatically alter the occupant's experience of a previously empty space. In doing so, the occupant is forced to become aware of how they move within the dwelling and the spatial limits it imposes. The presence and position of the objects it contains are also brought to the fore. As a result, all three aspects become inevitably intertwined and the resident experiences the space in a completely new way, thus exploring the concept of how the inhabitant interprets and uses small spaces for living.

Tasked to evoke questions of significance, the bold forms can be interpreted in a myriad of ways. Are they an abstraction of classical architectural elements? A sculptural piece in what might actually be considered a gallery? Or do they simply hold value only as functional objects, like pieces of furniture?

Perhaps their arrangement is justifiable simply as an innovative way to create spatial hierarchy in an apartment without walls, marking and defining different areas according to a specific domestic use—an entrance hall, a central living room, and a bedroom with a panoramic view. By moving the yellow objects, the resident has the power to redefine the spaces to their own taste, creating a sense of freedom and dynamism within the compact home environment, perhaps resulting in a design that provides a unique combination of contemplation and functionality.

"Tasked to evoke questions of significance, the dwelling's bold forms can be interpreted in a myriad of ways."

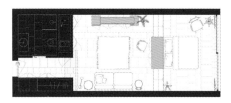

Floor plan

 2 4 6 9.84 ft
1 2 3 m

ARGENTONA APARTMENT

Barcelona, Spain
968 ft² (90 m²)
Design: YLAB Arquitectos
Photography: Tobias Laarmann

Dark, disconnected from the outside world, and heavily partitioned, this once dingy apartment is now unrecognizable thanks to great design. Located in a charming old building amid narrow, leaf-strewn streets in Barcelona's Gracia district, it has been transformed into a free-flowing, contemporary, and tastefully eclectic holiday home for the owners.

Covered with ivy vines, the courtyard—undoubtedly the property's best feature—floods the interior with natural light, and the owners sought to capitalize on this valuable aspect in the home's refurbishment. Reviving the previously static inner courtyard was at the heart of the design concept and it was transformed into a semi-exterior garden. Dotted with a selection of custom planters, it imparts vibrant greenery to the space and connects the dwelling with nature and the outside.

The overall, award-winning design is exciting and clever, outlining *and* at the same time concealing spaces and amenities with floor-to-ceiling cabinetry. Key areas comprise an en suite master bedroom laden with custom timber cabinetry that integrates a folding dresser; a stylish communal area; a kitchen with cooking and washing facilities that hide behind closed doors when not in use; breakfast and bar zones; and a refurbished courtyard/gallery.

> "This once dingy apartment has been transformed into a free-flowing, contemporary, and tastefully eclectic holiday home."

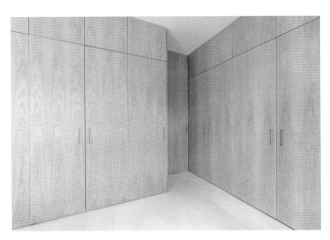

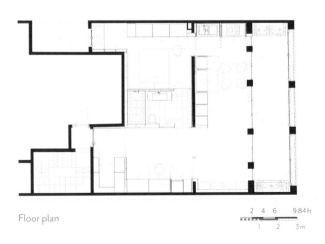

Floor plan

2 4 6   9.84 ft

1   2   3 m

Conceived as "the world in one room," this innovative design packs a space-saving punch thanks to its clever, kitted-out walls and a window that expands the perception of the space.

The idea for the design was to create a dynamic and concentrated living space that would be able to change its appearance through the day, in accordance with the occupants' desired use.

BATIPIN FLAT

Milan, Italy
301 ft² (28 m²)
Design: studio wok
Photography: Federico Villa

Multiple functional aspects and practical, yet comfortable living scenarios were achieved by creating two "active" walls that conceal all of the apartment's fixed furniture (including a fold-out bed), sliding doors to the bathroom and kitchen, a wardrobe, and a space for the air-conditioning unit. The kitchen and bathroom are presented as two monochrome teal-blue boxes hidden away from the main space, while the living area is characterized by white surfaces that amplify brightness and showcase the warmth and materiality of the wooden walls. Central to the apartment is a large window, which overlooks a terrace and adds a unique sense of aperture to the space. This layout, combined with its quirky, yet congenial aesthetics, affords impressive living flexibility while deterring the potential for small-space stagnation.

"Large apartment living condensed into a small studio space."

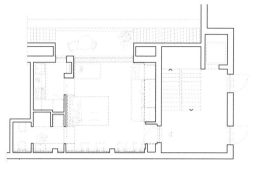

8:30 am: Wake up!

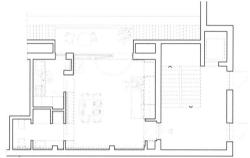

12:30 pm: Lunch time

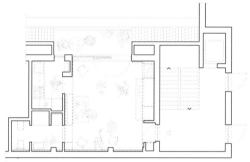

11:30 pm: Let's party!

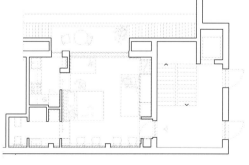

2:30 am: Sleeping time (with guests)

BEIRA MAR HOUSE

Aveiro, Portugal
1,410 ft² (131 m²)
Design: Paulo Martins
Arquitectura & Design
Photography: Ivo Tavares Studio

Located in an established Beira Mar neighborhood, this sophisticated residence captures the sound of seagulls, the smell of the sea breeze, and the colors of the sky and surrounding greenery. The result of a passionate yet challenging reform, the home intends to provide its occupants with a freeing lifestyle that remains in contact with the outdoors.

Built on a challengingly small plot of land that is long and narrow, it formally establishes itself as a habitable corridor, which, from the point of entry, is filled with accumulative moments of darkness, light, surprise, discovery, compression, and, lastly, release. With sober and elemental materials vying for attention throughout, basic and essential function areas are covered in concrete.

The building is clad protectively with plasterboard that is painted dark green, rigorously shielded for its new and invigorated lifecycle. Internally, the dwelling is dark and intimate. By conceptual and practical contrast, the exterior is a white and purposefully reflective surface that floods the house with light, sometimes diffused and soft, sometimes direct and intense.

Relative to design, all social functions have been planned to take place on the first floor, in direct contact with the backyard patio, while the upper floor, visually protected from unwanted eyes by a plant curtain, is reserved for the bedrooms and a solarium.

"A passionate yet challenging reform that provides its occupants with a freeing lifestyle in contact with the outdoors."

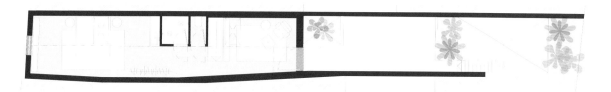

Second-floor plan

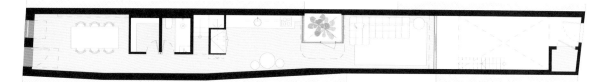

First-floor plan

2 4 6   9.84 ft
1   2   3 m

Suspended above a creek on a rural property outside of Adelaide, the aptly named Bridge House is unique and eye-catching. The owners wished for a home and office that celebrated the natural beauty of their small, but environmentally diverse property with a limited environmental footprint. The result is a narrow, compact, and unimposing form that peacefully sits among the trees.

BRIDGE HOUSE

Adelaide, South Australia, Australia
1,184 ft² (110 m²)
Design: Max Pritchard Architect
Photography: Sam Noonan

Four small concrete piers on each side of the creek anchor two steel trusses that hold up a concrete slab on steel decking with a layer of rigid insulation, forming the home's foundational structure. The interior is decorated with an unassuming muted palette, and is sparsely furnished, so as not to detract from the beauty outside. The long sides of the house facing north and south feature large windows to afford views of the natural scenery on each side, providing the occupants with the sense that they are living within the landscape.

In colder months, insulation to the underside of the slab floor, walls, and roof, combined with double-glazed curtained windows aid in the retention of heat; the insulated concrete flooring radiates it out at night. A small wood combustion heater fuelled by timber grown sustainably on the site provides additional warmth when required.

In summer, pressed steel screens shade the sun-drenched north-facing windows, while a combination of ceiling fans and operable windows efficiently and effectively cool the interior through cross ventilation. Taking sustainability a step further, roof water is collected for use within the house and photovoltaic cells located on an adjacent shed provide power. The result is a splendid combination of an environmentally friendly residence with access to views of the outside, perfectly designed to fit in its small location.

"A narrow, compact, and unimposing form that peacefully sits among the trees."

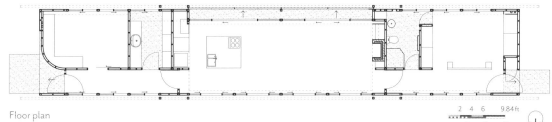

Floor plan

This once boxy apartment with an excessive distribution of space now resembles a modern and multifunctional haven for a father and son. The clever design concept optimizes the minimal space on offer, while still providing a spacious living area, a bathroom, and two bedrooms.

BUTTES CHAUMONT

Paris, France
753 ft² (70 m²)
Design: Glenn Medioni Agency
Photography: Pascal Otlinghaus

At the heart of the design is a "principal room," which acts as the main living space. Bordering one side of the living area, a slatted, wooden feature wall conceals the bedrooms and bathroom. Dramatically contrasting with this muted principal space is a bold, statement piece that acts as a "hub." Intended as a large cabinet for regrouping and combining lifestyle amenities, which include an office space, the television, and storage, this eye-catching configuration is a practical addition to the space that also injects some fun dynamism with its white visage and bright yellow niches.

The same multifunctional design module with its exciting pops of yellow is imitated in the son's bedroom. Just as in the principal room structure, a bed, desk space, and ample storage are all integrated into a single form, allowing for plenty of floor space to satisfy the need for all-important playtime.

"A once boxy apartment turned modern and multifunctional haven for a father and son."

43

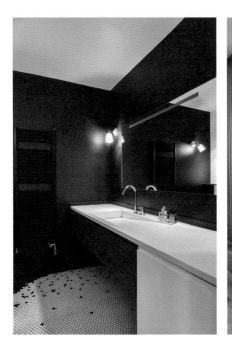

Floor plan

2 4 6 9.84 ft
1 2 3 m

Fed up with the modern-day society's obsessive pursuit of "things" rather than lived experiences, the cabin's creator set out to create an antidote to what he quips is a "craziness we've brought upon ourselves."

CABN JUDE

Adelaide, South Australia, Australia
160 ft² (15 m²)
Design: Michael Lamprell
Photography: Dylan Minchenberg

"The basic human instinct of interaction is being diminished by a society more comfortable with banter on social media than real-world encounters. We get greater satisfaction from possessions than we do from heartfelt experiences."

Designed to provide people with a much-needed digital detox, this small, completely off-grid, sustainable, and ecofriendly cabin, ideally located in South Australia's stunning Adelaide Hills, allows residents to become re-acquainted with the natural environment and their place within it. Set in natural scrubland, it is adjacent to a conservation park with incredible walking trails, creeks, dams, and breathtaking scenery—the ideal setting to neutralize today's technology-laden lifestyles.

The innovative interior design includes space for a king-size bed, toilet, shower, heater, two-burner kitchen stove, full-size sink, and fridge. The interior is clad with light-colored wood, which helps to enhance the sense of space. Large windows bring in plenty of natural light, while the clever design means everything the resident needs is within easy reach.

An abundance of surrounding trees and adjustable windows keep the site cool, ensuring that the cabin can also be enjoyed during the summer months. The nearby forest, creeks, waterfalls, and bushwalking tracks, as well as a wealth of wildlife—including kangaroos, bandicoots, and plenty of birdlife—make for a truly immersive experience.

"The clever design means everything one needs is within easy reach."

This compact vacation home is immersed in southeastern Mexico's wild landscape. Designed for a pair of young adults, the objective was to achieve a reflective and contemplative place that links the occupants with the surrounding environment. The result is an intuitive, functional, and simple living experience that offers great spatial warmth.

CASA DE MONTE

Mexico
452 ft² (42 m²)
Design: TACO taller de
arquitectura contextual
Photography: Leo Espinosa

Past the doors, an open terrace commands the eye and leads the gaze out to the pool and outdoor area. The interior is a double-height space that houses a kitchenette and living room and a staircase that ascends to a mezzanine bedroom. Beneath the mezzanine is storage and closet space, a bathroom with an outdoor shower, and an exterior staircase that leads to the entrance.

Both the interior and exterior are finished in rough stucco with artisanal paint based on lime and mineral pigments. This striking but warm textural appearance mimics the rocky soil that shoulders the dwelling, subtly weaving the impression that the architecture naturally manifested within the landscape.

"An intuitive, functional, and simple living experience with great spatial warmth."

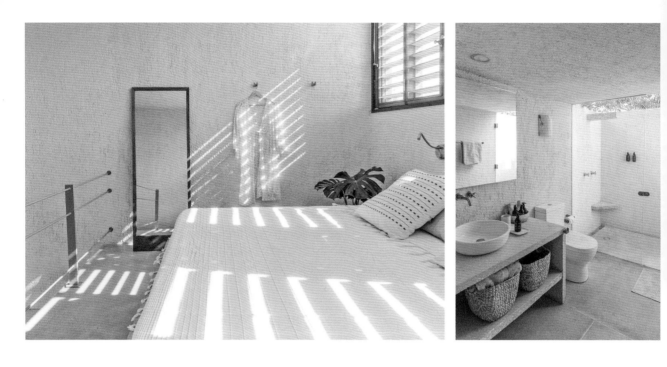

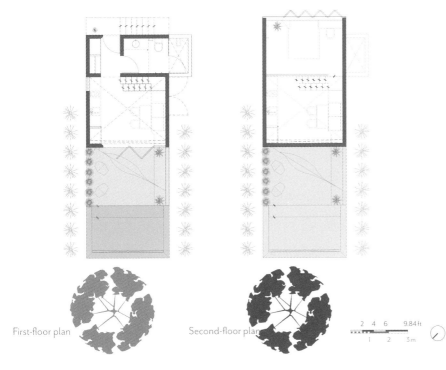

First-floor plan   Second-floor plan

2 4 6   9.84 ft
1   2   3 m

CASA PARASITO

San Juan, Ecuador
129 ft² (12 m²)
Design: El Sindicato Arquitectura
Photography: Andrés Villota and
Paolo Caicedo

More a minimal design object rather than a house, Casa Parasito effortlessly provides accommodations for two people in a cleverly unique location: the rooftop of a city building in San Juan. In using such an underused, but structurally sound space, the architects wanted to not only provide a home but also to contribute positively to the densification challenge faced by the city's inhabitants.

The design concept hinges on an A-frame façade. Within, an interior layout is marked by a rectangular core—also the main social/living space—from which all other utilitarian spaces, such as the kitchen, dining table, bathroom, bed, work area, and storage are accessed. These utilitarian services, adjacent to the core at either ends of the structure, are situated within triangles and rhomboids.

A large transparent window allows natural light to filter through into the interior. Orientated toward the north, Casa Parasito opens out to views of the city and the Cotacachi, Imbabura, Mojanda, and Cayambe volcanoes. The south façade is laden with frosted glass to ensure illumination, ventilation, and privacy for the residents.

"A minimal design object that solves basic habitation needs and positively contributes to the densification of a city."

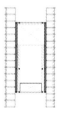

Second-floor plan

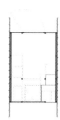

First-floor plan

In a row of workers' cottages stands a dark horse. Its architectural characteristics—stepped parapet, centered window, and entrance awning—maintain the same unassuming composure of the neighboring properties. But its stark, twenty-first-century outfit gives away the contemporary home that hides within.

DARK HORSE

Melbourne, Victoria, Australia
1,399 ft² (130 m²)
Design: Architecture Architecture
Photography: Peter Bennetts

A palette of black, white, and gray flows through the house, highlighting and downplaying spaces to lend tonal variation and spatial depth. Spaces expand and contract in this color-play to define social areas, cozy nooks, and recreational zones for the resident to enjoy. In the living areas, where space and light are abundant, the palette is darker, creating spaces for comfortable repose. In the corridors where space is tighter, the palette lightens and the ceilings lift. The corridor walls—slim and prefabricated to maximize internal space—are lined with a metal sheet to reflect light deep into the house.

The living areas in the house open onto a courtyard, forming the sunlit heart of the house, around which daily human activity plays out. Upstairs, timber floors and lining boards set a warmer tone for sleep and rest areas. Dramatic skylights and generous windows cast this dark horse in abundant natural light as it gallops into the modern world of small homes.

"Familiar and unassuming in composition but highly contemporary in character."

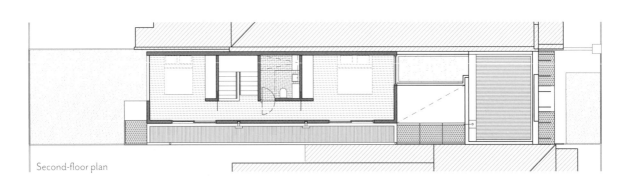

Second-floor plan

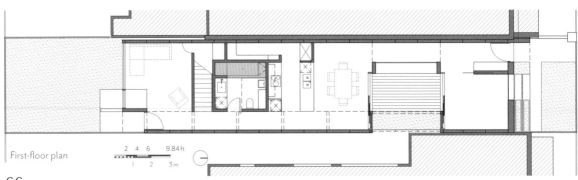

First-floor plan

2 4 6   9.84 ft
1   2   3 m

In architect Sjuul Cluitmans's opinion, lofts tend to be the most spacious of housing type, exuding the most contemporary style. He believes that the loft typology translates well to small spaces— as Egons Loft located in the north of Amsterdam so artfully demonstrates. Here, architect and furniture designer collaborate to use the width of the small space to their utmost advantage to create a comfortable and one-of-a-kind home.

EGONS LOFT

Amsterdam, The Netherlands
484 ft² (45 m²)
Design: Heren 5 Architects
Interior build and design: Paul Timmer
Photography: Tim Stet and
Leonard Faustle

A large glass façade overlooks the canal below, creating a feeling of spaciousness thanks to the integrated outdoor views. Communal living areas, such as the kitchen and dining nook, are cleverly orientated behind this glass face, maximizing the width of the apartment. Inviting in views of the outside so seamlessly creates a welcome feeling of spaciousness in these modest living quarters. Storage space and the bathroom are situated at the back of the loft, while the sleeping area is located on top of the kitchen, made possible by an extra-high ceiling.

Central to the apartment is a large interior unit (with diamond-edged detailing) that absorbs the stove area, provides storage, and attaches the stairs to the sleeping area. Made from a subtle palette of birch and white Corian, this in-built functional form further softens the interior while giving it a dynamic feel.

"The loft typology tends to be the most spacious and translates well to small spaces."

71

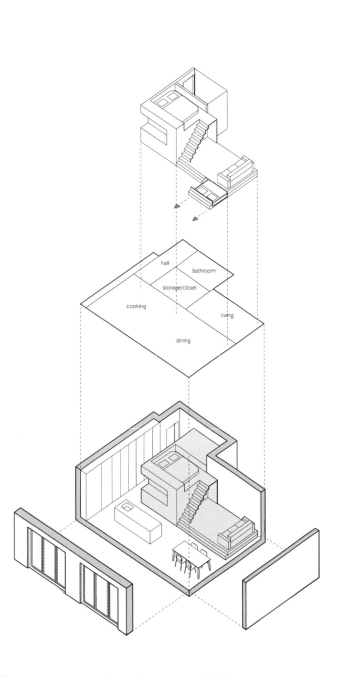

hall

bathroom

storage/closet

cooking

living

dining

FLEXSE

St Petersburg, Russia
328 ft² (30.5 m²)
Design: SA lab
Photography: Ekaterina Titenko

A modern take on a Scandinavian grill house, FLEXSE is a sophisticated micro dwelling with an impressive list of seasonal adaptations. A cozy and comfortable modular house, it's the ideal place to retreat into during the winter months, given its cubby-hole ambiance. During the warmer climates, cuddling up inside can be exchanged for lounging in the open terrace outside.

FLEXSE maximizes usable area while maintaining a modest footprint and a strong sense of versatility. Though the first prototype was used as a small grill house, its modular adaptability can be tailored for different purposes: a sauna, a guest dwelling, and even a complete tiny house. The design also has potential as a café, shop, or innovative office space. It's this customizable format, inside and out, that takes the idea of living little that one big step further.

It is made of 100 percent recyclable materials and can be assembled in parts on-site, or be positioned on different foundations. These include concrete slabs and metal piers, which allows for placement in remote areas, the countryside, and even on water. Its main features include an angled roof to minimize the accumulation of snow, a prominent wood-stripped interior and exterior, and an open grill that warms the space. Moreover, the large, circular window and glazed doors let in natural light and allow the occupant to enjoy the surrounding scenery.

"A tiny house, sauna or inner-city office space? FLEXSE is all of the above."

Barbecue house

Shop

Gallery

Café/bar

Lounge zone

Tiny cabin

Guest house

Sauna

GLASSHOUSE TREEHOUSE

Catskills Mountains, NY, United States
120 ft² (11 m²)
Design: ElevenTwoEleven Design
Photography: courtesy
ElevenTwoEleven Design

The Glasshouse Treehouse is a DIY project of interior designer Christina Salway, who artfully captures and reinterprets the charm of a greenhouse in the treetops of New York State's verdant Catskills. The space's whimsical location in the trees offers the occupants vantage points to appreciate views of the surrounding property from above, and its unique position and character make this lingering treehouse a magical place to rest and work in.

Planning began by salvaging windows discarded on street corners and rescuing similar cast-offs from antique stores. Friends and family were also approached to donate any unwanted or unused doors and windows. The inspiration was to create a "patchwork quilt" of collected, gifted, and found pieces, to add to the sentimental charm of the dwelling. This collage design expands on the panoramic views of the countryside and allows for a more intimate connection with the surrounding outdoors.

Taking up only a very small space, the treehouse gracefully unravels into three primary zones: a work area, a sleeping area, and a lounge. Each area exists independently but is configured to allow occupants to both flow between them with ease and use them collectively. The thoughtful curation of objects—eliminating the superfluous that are neither functional nor meaningful—makes the most of space in such tight quarters. There is still room, however, for fun. A slide pole installed off the deck invites a youthful and carefree shimmy down, keeping the spirit as elevated as the home it resides in.

"A magical place to work and rest that lingers in the treetops of the Catskills Mountains."

Floor plan

2 4 6   9.84 ft

1 2 3 m

GOLDFIELDS DWELLING

Chewton, Victoria, Australia
1,076 ft² (100 m²)
Design: DesignOffice
Photography: Scottie Cameron

On an expansive property in the heart of Victoria's Goldfields region, sits a small and unassuming home. This small home is an artwork of elegant simplicity with contextual consideration.

Clad in warm, gray asphalt shingles, the pavilion-form house settles tactfully into its leafy surrounds. Inside, the compact dwelling accommodates two bedrooms ("stacked" on top of one another), an open kitchen, and dining and living area. Orientated beneath the apex of the building, the airy living space enjoys generous ceiling height, which gives an otherwise neat area a lofty, light-filled ambiance. This atmosphere is enhanced by interiors that are defined with a calming, minimal-material palette: concrete flooring, white oak joinery, and ceramic tiles.

Large windows placed on each face of the house create sightlines throughout, allowing abundant natural light to filter in as they provide the inhabitants with continuous views of the idyllic rural site. This generous use of glazing, coupled with skylights, projects a sense of spaciousness beyond the pavilion's small footprint. The main living area in the west mitigates and matches the facing site's sloping topography through a tiered, timber outfit that embraces a cozy if modest space for human interaction and relaxation.

"An exercise in elegant simplicity and contextual consideration in the Victorian Goldfields."

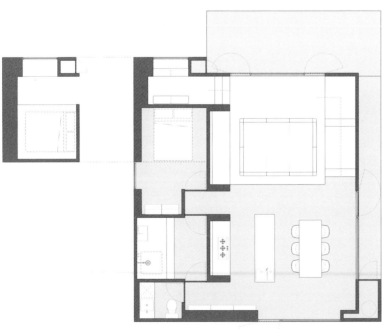

Floor plan

2 4 6   9.84 ft

1 2   3m

GRAN DE GRACIA MINI APARTMENT

Barcelona, Spain
409 ft² (38 m²)
Design: YLAB Arquitectos
Photography: Tobias Laarmann

It's difficult to imagine this warm and versatile apartment in its former state as the once rundown residence of the building's gatekeeper. This once-dilapidated dwelling has since been given new life and turned into an occasional Barcelona-based residence for the owners. Ideally located on a rooftop in Barcelona's elegant Gracia district, it is surrounded by a large terrace and enjoys a privileged view, overlooking neighboring buildings and the city below.

The design concept completely reforms the interior to achieve a stylish, comfortable, and functional dwelling that prioritizes day spaces. A central hub formed by the kitchen and living area organizes the flow of activities in the apartment during the day.

In the evening, this space transitions into a bedroom with a pull-down bed masterfully integrated into the wall cabinets. Light and easy-to-move pieces, such as Paulistano lounge chairs, a Marset floor lamp, and a Muuto table, furnish the space and bring out its easy-going nature.

The walls and ceiling are covered with custom-made carpentry that alternates white satin lacquer with natural light-oak veneer. This perimeter carpentry provides abundant storage and also forms functional elements that optimize the apartment, such as the neatly concealed writing desk that pulls out for a minimalist office. Beyond functional duties, this woodwork also unifies and refines the overall interior to create a small, warm and luminous dwelling in which many details are cleverly veiled by a pure and simple image.

"A small, warm, and luminous dwelling in which many details are cleverly veiled by a pure and simple image."

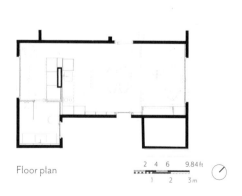

Floor plan

2 4 6   9.84 ft
1   2   3 m

GRANNY PAD

Seattle, Washington, United States
571 ft² (53 m²)
Design: Best Practice Architecture
Photography: Ed Sozinho

This savvy, artfully tailored space is for an aging family member who lives in a city with painfully limited housing options. Here, the granny pad is redefined.

The innovative residential addition was built to give the family member a safe and well-designed dwelling and to bring childcare to a growing family; all the while maintaining privacy for everyone involved. In addition to meeting the immediate needs of the family, the space also needed to accommodate future use as a rental unit, studio, or office. Converting an existing garage (previously used as storage) was the perfect solution.

Rather than make several small rooms, the focus was to create open, central spaces that could be easily adapted to the changing mobility issues of an aging person.

A cozy yard at the front creates an inviting atmosphere and welcomes the resident into a warm, surprisingly spacious interior, courtesy of a high ceiling. Carefully placed windows and skylights provide lots of daylight, while exposed rafters create a loft-like atmosphere. A short walk through the entryway reveals the bedroom, bathroom, and laundry room. A lofted space above the bathroom (accessed by a ladder) can be used as storage, an office, or sleeping quarters. It also opens to a private back deck. All of these details come together to create an inviting, open-concept accommodations, making the relatively small footprint of this granny pad feel much larger than it really is.

"Rather than make several small rooms, the focus was to create open, central spaces that could be easily adapted to the changing mobility issues of an aging person."

Mezzanine floor plan

First-floor plan

2 4 6   9.84 ft

1   2   3 m

A complete refurbishment plus extension saw this dark, dated, and claustrophobic mews house transformed into a contemporary and carefree dwelling. By incorporating folding walls, mirrors, hidden storage, and a large skylight, the most has been made of a compact space, creating a home that is now bright, fresh, and well-suited to family life.

HACKNEY MEWS HOUSE

Greater London, United Kingdom
968 ft² (90 m²)
Design: HUTCH design
Photography: Helen Cathcart

With a reconfigured interior layout arranged over three split levels, a lively and dynamic environment is created. On the base level, an open-plan kitchen connects to the living and dining spaces to encourage family interaction and facilitate an easy sweep of the eye. The home office, which also doubles as a third bedroom, opens up to the living area by way of a bespoke, custom-built folding wall.

The reimagining of the layout into a continuous, open-plan arrangement creates a welcoming home; provides extra accommodations and storage for a growing family; modernizes the home from it's formerly sad, dilapidated state; and utilizes and maximizes the small space as much as possible. At the same time the spaces are flexible and multifunctional enough to meet the growing, varying needs of a family.

"A clever reconfiguration of compact space transforms a typical mews house into a lively and dynamic living environment."

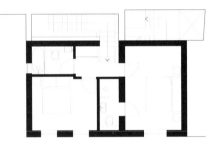

Second-floor plan

First-floor plan

2 4 6   9.84ft
1 2 3m

HOUSE MM

Amsterdam, The Netherlands
646 ft² (60 m²)
Design: Chris Collaris Architects
Photography: Tim Van de Velde

Despite its relatively small floor area, this contemporary home in north Amsterdam boasts significant internal volume. A once old and decaying brick house has been transformed by using every inch of the allocation plan to the new home's advantage—made possible by the clever mitigation of restricted roof heights. The outcome is an increase in volume that results in a spacious interior.

An exaggerated gabled roof cantilever over the lower exterior of the main building volume allowed the upper level of the house to be enlarged, enabling high ceilings on every floor and a useful attic space. A bonus being the sheltered path leading to the main entrance.

Finished with a protective wax-coated pinewood cladding in black, the home's exterior is clean-lined and makes a bold statement, standing out almost brazenly among its more mellow peers. This timber cladding yields only in precise areas for large windows throughout that invite light in and present delightful views, with full-height glazing that opens onto a terrace overlooking the gardens.

Though the new home flaunts a compelling and completely different character from its ancestor, the old brick house is not completely lost. The garden links ties to the past with a large, quirky planter fashioned from the old house's roof tiles. In the interior, reclaimed bricks grace a central brick core that separates different zones on the first floor, also adding a layer of rustic charm to this modern remake. An adjoining staircase works with this brick core to neatly divide the space into kitchen, dining area, and living room. The space under the staircase is maximized through a sweep of cabinetry in birch multiplex (plywood) that extends the home's timber accents while providing plenty of storage, accentuating the spacious proportions of this small home.

"Despite a small floor area, this contemporary home skilfully negotiates three stories within a two-story structure."

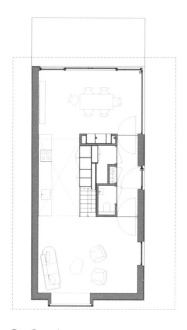

First-floor plan

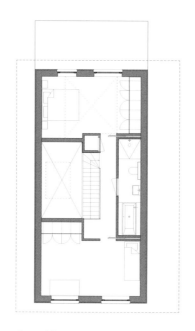

Second-floor plan

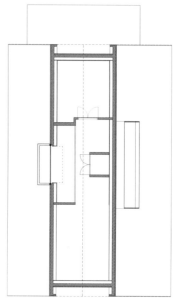

Third-floor plan

LA COLOMBIÈRE

Sutton, Quebec, Canada
1,300 ft² (120 m²)
Design: YH2 Architecture
Photography: Francis Pelletier

Once used as a storage shed by a lumberman, La Colombière now exists as an immersive forest retreat. Central to the design process was a commitment to preserving the surrounding landscape, and thereby limiting the building extension to the existing modest footprint. Inspired by the natural growth of trees, the design philosophy projects the dwelling as inextricably linked to the soil upon which it resides. As a result, all construction grew vertically, developing an aerial volume reminiscent of tree canopies.

These principles allowed for an extension without the sacrifice of trees or use of heavy machinery, both of which would have disrupted the natural environment. The dark cedar exterior further honors the landscape, paying homage to the surrounding conifers. Inside, the soaring ceiling and walls are painted white and materials from the existing building are retained and uninterrupted, emphasizing the new structure as an extension rather than an insertion.

On the first floor, a simple space unabashedly exposes the lush forest around, guiding a soulful connection between humankind and nature. On the upper floors, rooms washed in white are attired in the barest of trimmings, ensuring the outdoors takes centerstage, lovingly framed by large windows. Each room opens into a vast, vertical shaft punctured by a stairwell that leads to a nature-lover's dream on the top floor—an exterior, covered terrace that presents a cozy perch from where occupants can enjoy the compelling quietude of the forest.

"An aerially inclined refuge reminiscent of bird huts tucked away in the forest canopy."

First-floor plan

Second-floor plan

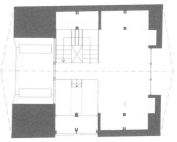

Third-floor plan

A 280-square-foot apartment isn't exactly what most have in mind when chasing down dreams of a life in the Big Apple, but it came to be anyway. Past the initial aversion, however, this Manhattan unit was soon transformed from an inappreciable hole in the wall to what the realtors dubbed "a beautifully renovated pre-war corner penthouse."

MANHATTAN HOLE IN THE WALL

New York City, New York, United States
280 ft² (26 m²)
Design: Gabrielle Savoie
Photography: Sean Litchfield

With an arsenal of small-space solutions, Marie Kondo–style decluttering philosophies, and ruthless design decisions, the homeowner learned to love living little in a tiny space, and made it *normal*.

The first and hardest step was a non-negotiable culling of clutter. Trial-and-error floor planning with ideas drawn to scale on architectural software formed the next phase; five months later, a layout to make a home of this tiny hole in the wall was finally confirmed.

Thoughtfully selected décor pieces, such as attractive sconces, cozy rugs in a favorite color or even admired artwork make the space relatable and feel instantly homey—something a first-time small-home resident will appreciate. Window treatments are not passed over either. In this small space, opaque solar shades have become smart investments that protect privacy, yet let ample light through with their thin material. Assortments of personal items take refuge in baskets under the bed while the television stand doubles as a dresser and storage. Kitchen cabinets also creatively provide storage for more than just crockery to maximize every area possible. Making it all fit *as one sees fit* is a good approach when tackling such a small space. Albeit compact, this tiny but cozy, personalized unit audibly croons "home sweet home."

"How big?" I asked again. He flinched: "280 square feet." Was that even legal?

Floor plan

2   4   6   9.84 ft

1   2   3 m

PARLAMENT19

Barcelona, Spain
700 ft² (65 m²)
Design: Miel Arquitectos and Studio P10
Photography: Jose Hevia and Asier Rua

An experiment in reflective ergonomics, Parlament19 was inspired by a creative distribution of mirrors that entices glimmers of light into the third floor of the Sant Antonio apartment block in which it resides. This strategy was applied when designing the apartment's internal distribution of space. What resulted was the careful positioning of a cube of mirrors, which act as a geometric hinge, sending a kaleidoscope of light throughout the apartment.

This golden cube houses specific services that can be utilized without natural light—the kitchen and two en suite bathrooms. Externally, it creates an illusion of space that spreads to the bedrooms and communal areas. Upon entering the apartment, it acts as a gatehouse inviting the visitor into its magnified surroundings.

Carefully balanced, the overall layout rotates around the centrally boxed kitchen and bathrooms. It consists of a living/dining room and balcony, adjacent to a bedroom with en suite. The final area, situated in the quieter internal mezzanine, consists of a bedroom, office/dining room, and bathroom. Through a combination of sliding doors and curtains the space connects and disconnects from the rest of the apartment, making it easy for occupants to adapt to social or intimate functions. A deliberate smattering of gold and gold-hued accents with structural reinforcements—door handles, switches, ceiling fissures—add warmth and luminosity to the space.

The element of surprise is a wonderful tool to enrich and rediscover, particularly when employed in a domestic space.

"An experiment in reflective ergonomics that enriches a domestic space."

Floor plan

PINE FLAT

Bordeaux, France
527 ft² (49 m²)
Design: A6A
Photography: Agnès Clotis

Defined by an abundance of warm timber accents and an overall sense of intrigue, the aptly named Pine Flat resides inconspicuously on the top floor of a nineteenth-century building. Full of innovative design ideas, it showcases the architect's ingenious and effective use of the small space available.

The result is an interior with a layered feel to it. The space is made up of different platforms, partitions, doors, and storage stitched together by plywood installations contrasting harmoniously against the white, loft-style ceiling. The color and texture of veined wood patterns against the white of the beams, walls, and ceilings, plus the soft gray of the kitchen attractively disguise the size of the interior. They also create a warm, yet contemporary atmosphere suited for the modern day. Adding to the apartment's congenial feel are heightened windows on the west side, which bathe the space in natural light while also offering views of two contrasting buildings: the bell tower of the Saint Paul Church, built in the seventeenth century, and the roof of the Palais des Sport, a recently renovated glass and concrete work from the brutalist movement of the 1960s.

These architectural "injections" give the apartment a dynamic, two-dimensional feel while capitalizing on limited space. They also create intriguing sight lines for the occupants. The overall effect is a cozy and modern space, where the warmth of pine wood glows in the abundant daylight.

"At the top of a nineteenth-century building, glimpses of natural daylight lead to a small but welcoming front door."

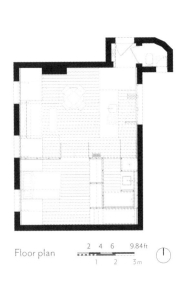

Floor plan

2 4 6 9.84 ft
1 2 3 m

A smidgen, let alone an entire wall of fluorescent green, isn't a design choice that necessarily bodes well when living little, but this apartment design proves that small spaces can be bold, bright, and aesthetically busy.

Designed as a tourist apartment for short but vibrant stays, this Barcelona flat was bravely reformed to become an exciting social temple. The two bedrooms in all white breathe a strong sense of calm and boast innovative designs. Re-purposing of old materials and removing part of the existing brick have afforded a clever configuration that allows a built-in wardrobe and desk space in each room. To further maximize the use of space, all piping and wiring are enclosed in a platform timber floor, which also gives the interior an interesting elevated aspect. Residing on this elevation is the kitchen, which is wrapped with a bar, providing an inviting place for residents to chat and have a munch.

A prominent aspect of the apartment's design is the large mirrored wall that sits opposite the kitchen. This wall pulls double duty: presenting doorways that lead to the bathroom while reflecting light from the window into the main living space and kitchen. The interior is further illuminated by eclectic PET Lamps by Alvaro Catalán de Ocón, which hang casually throughout.

PISO PEREIV44

Barcelona, Spain
645 ft² (60 m²)
Design: Miel Arquitectos
Photography: Asier Rua

"The kitchen is more like a raised DJ booth than Grandma's cozy cooking corner."

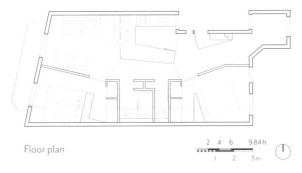

Floor plan

2 4 6   9.84 ft
1   2   3 m

POD-IDLADLA

Johannesburg, South Africa
183 ft² (17 m²)
Design: Clara da Cruz Almeida
Architect CC
Interior and furnishing: Dokter
And Misses
Photography: Brett Rubin

With a strong focus on cost-effectiveness, space-saving strategies, and adaptability, POD-iDladla is a transportable nano home only 183 square feet (17 square meters) in size. Made and manufactured in South Africa, the home's name iDladla means "my place" in Johannesburg's urban slang.

This pod is transportable from place to place (creating a colorful variety of home bases), or left in one location to be leased out. This nifty invention is part of a project that aims to encourage a new synergy between house and landowner, while also providing the option for mobility in a fast-moving society. A strong focus on adaptability also ensures a range of future use options that include a possible studio space, rented cottage, or holiday unit. Furthermore, its modular structure can be demounted or added to, forming multiple variations that expand its potential.

Inside, the design implements a variety of space-saving strategies: a double volume to create passive ventilation and a sense of spaciousness; a covered outdoor living area; and a shower positioned in a passage. The loft-like layout also manages a bed on the top level and a kitchen and office space on the bottom. Crisp white walls with pops of color and timber accents line the interior and ensure that an otherwise micro space feels warm, open, and easy to navigate.

"A transportable nano home with a focus on cost-effectiveness, space-saving strategies, and adaptability."

PRIVATE
APARTMENT
IN MILAN

Milan, Italy
323 ft² (30 m²)
Design: untitled architecture
Photography: Giovanni Emilio Galanello

Located in the attic of an old residential building in Milan, this apartment features a strong vertical connection that is key to its design. A tubular, semi-cylindrical column of stairs composed in three different elements—natural marble at the start, steel in the middle, and timber at the end—resides at the heart of the interior. Its curved form creates a vivid contrast with the rigid geometry of the rest of the apartment, while its supporting sheath, proportionately designed, emphasizes the vertical continuity of the internal space.

Cabinetry installed along the internal perimeter frees up as much space as possible in this small-scale apartment and maintains the theme of spatial continuity. It also defines the kitchen area, housing a sink and an oven, and provides welcome storage for the residents. The choice of materials has been kept very neutral in order to highlight the irregular geometry of the apartment. Rough white plaster, oak flooring, and blonde timber furniture are prominent anchors in the space. The same materials call out from various, sometimes, opposing surfaces, such as the oak countertop in the bathroom, which is in fact, also the flooring. In that vein, the sliding door is shaped from the same wood as the furniture. The bathroom too makes its own statement. The white, square tiles feature bold, blue grout, which ties back to the blue frame of the stairs. This mimicking of design impressions and materials on surfaces achieves strong visual integrity throughout the dwelling while changing the perception of an otherwise cramped space.

"Spatial continuity and visual integrity alter the perception of an otherwise cramped space."

First-floor plan

Second-floor plan

2 4 6   9.84 ft
1   2   3 m

With a lakeside setting reminiscent of an all-American summer camp movie, this quintessential Washington cabin is nestled deep within a temperate rainforest. It retains a romantic sense of history while obliging subtle alignment with contemporary aesthetics. Once belonging to a violin maker, it bears several original features, making it easy to imagine a bygone era within its walls. In an attempt to

QUINAULT CABIN

Washington, United States
750 ft² (70 m²)
Design: Best Practice Architecture
Photography: Mark Woods

preserve a prominent sense of history and reflect twenty-first-century design sensibilities, the pursuit of a thoughtful restoration weaves a modern twist without compromising the character of the interior.

Completely remodeled, the internal layout comprises two bedrooms, a living space with an adjoining deck, and a bathroom. The original wood stove was relocated to turn what were once bedrooms into a living space that faces the lake and connects to the outdoor deck. The old bathroom was enlarged and modernized to include a shower, and the bedrooms updated with contemporary vanities for the convenience of guests. By emphasizing period features and introducing found objects, the quintessential "cabin vibe" is successfully retained as it is skillfully combined with unassuming modish elements.

"Once belonging to a violin maker, the romantic history of this all-American cabin lingers."

Floor plan

2 4 6   9.84 ft
1   2   3 m

SALVA46

Barcelona, Spain
527 ft² (49 m²)
Design: Miel Arquitectos and
Studio P10
Photography: Asier Rua

What happens when inventive architects experiment with shared micro-living concepts? A space in which movement and fluidity contrast with privacy and stability.

This innovative creation achieves the much sought-after balance between physiological and mental wellbeing, *plus* flexible co-existence. Much like the twenty-first-century nomadic lifestyle tendencies that inspired its design, the end product can be considered a play of opposites in a world of conformists.

Salva46 is an ingenious approach that almost combines two apartments into one unit. It comprises two independent sections, each housing four zones tending to the basic requirements of sleep, work, relaxation, and hygiene. Both these sections share access to a central common space containing the kitchen, dining, and social area. The idea of living little in a shared space might sound daunting but this residence achieves a precise relationship between crisp design and privacy. Individual personal quarters can be enclosed and secured without blocking the traverse of natural light, enabling quiet time to catch up on work or get lost in a book. At night, solid sliding doors cocoon each unit for complete escape into rest mode.

A high ceiling injects a dynamic sense of space to the apartments and affords two multipurpose mezzanines that levitate over the beds in each section, creating extra space for storage or a lounging nook. Relaxed furniture pieces made from timber, stone, and metal create balance and complete the micro-living experience.

"A play of opposites
in a world of conformists."

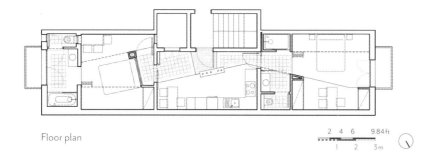

Floor plan

SAN JUAN TINY HOUSE

Colorado, United States
280 ft² (26 m²)
Design: Rocky Mountain Tiny Houses
Photography: Greg Parham

High in the Colorado Mountains, this completely off-grid home cleverly fuses art and functionality. Home to a young couple and their two dogs, the eye-catching dwelling showcases the impeccable craftsmanship and creative flair of its occupants (the human variety, of course). Builders themselves, they are also tiny-house enthusiasts who took pains to construct their San Juan tiny house all on their own. Externally striking, some of the home's notable features include a wavy roof; angled front prowl; barn wood siding arranged in a sunray pattern; blue ombré shakes on the rear wall; reclaimed materials throughout; and a collapsible front porch, which features a fold-up deck and fold-down awning (made from solar panels that tuck into the house when on the move).

On the inside, plenty of clever solutions maximize square feet and storage. The living area doubles as the primary sleeping area via an elevator bed that stores high during the day and lowers down at night. The couple's previous tiny house posed somewhat of a challenge with a cramped sleeping loft, which was difficult to access by a ladder. Therefore, for this build, a downstairs sleeping arrangement was crucial. A wood mural adorns the bottom of the bed frame, incorporating some art, while engaging the eye with something interesting to look at when the bed is raised. Other prominent design elements include the turquoise inlaid mesquite counters, art nouveau–inspired French doors, and the unique, multifunctioning woodworking details throughout.

"A hand-built, completely off-grid home that cleverly fuses art and functionality."

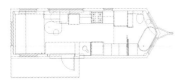

Floor plan

2 4 6 9.84ft
1 2 3m

SEASIDE HOUSE

Les Portes-en-Ré, France
3,444 ft² (320 m²)
Design: Martins Afonso Atelier Design
Photography: Mickaël Martins Afonso

Nestled in the seaside just north of France's Île de Ré, this dynamic dwelling stands surrounded by a beautiful garden. The home opens up on every side, multiplying perspectives and revealing itself through a range of sequences and views. The spaces eagerly come to life as each architectural fragment emerges within its context.

The owners sought to renovate the dwelling such that it aligned with their tastes, lifestyle, and desired comfort levels; and by redefining the interior and its relationship with the outdoors. Changes were very carefully considered to create functional links between rooms and to establish unique relations with the outdoors, all within a compact and modest floor plan. This sequencing work is defined and highlighted through the use of solid wood, which forms a common denominator throughout the home.

Solid oak woodwork connects two living rooms, a dining room, and a kitchen. These central spaces also outline area sequences and offer scenic frames of the outside, which highlight the exterior context and invite it indoors. These design aspects, in addition to detailed carpentry and materials such as terra cotta, create a lovely sense of warmth within the space, encouraging its occupants to relax and appreciate the tranquil atmosphere.

"The home opens up on every side, multiplying perspectives and revealing itself through a range of sequences and views."

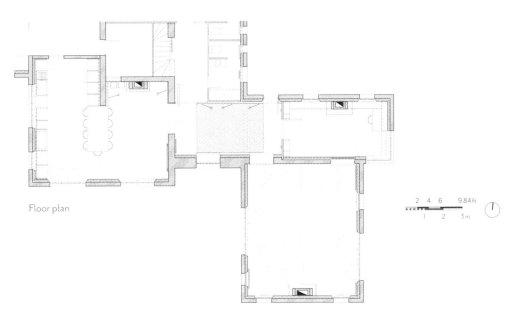

Floor plan

2 4 6 9.84 ft
1 2 3 m

Essentially a blank canvas, Senri Apartments is an innovative concept designed to emphasize individuality and accommodate a wide variety of lifestyles. The idea is for the resident's use of the space and their arrangement of personal items to build each dwelling and imbue it with personalized uniqueness.

SENRI APARTMENTS

Osaka, Japan
592 ft² (55 m²)
Design: nmstudio architects and
Nozoe Shimpei Architects
Photography: Koji Okumura
(Forward Stroke Inc.)

Central to the design of each unit is a wooden structure known as Shima. The Shima replaces existing partition walls and acts as a piece of multifunctional furniture that gently divides the space. It can also present as a wall to display loved knickknacks; can be optimized as a coat hanger or bookshelf; and can even be re-purposed as a day-bed for an afternoon nap or a reading nook to enjoy a relaxing time-out. This unique design allows residents to freely modify the space as they please, utilizing the Shima in their own individualistic way.

Curtains attached to the Shima enable a clear division of space, giving the impression of separate rooms. Its raised platform (12 inches [30 centimeters] from the floor) creates room for the imagination to play: it can be turned it into a cozy corner for social gatherings with the use of cushions, or fashioned into a Japanese-style dining area where the section hollows out at the base. The section with shelves may be used as a desk or closet space. In addition to its multiple applications, the Shima includes plenty of concealed storage with a spacious underfloor compartment that keeps excesses and clutter away and out of sight, for streamlined minimalist living.

"The arrangement of residents' belongings determines the identity of each dwelling."

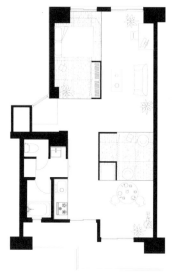

Floor plan (type A1)

Floor plan (type A2)

| 2 | 4 | 6 | 9.84 ft |
| 1 | 2 | 3 m |

Floor plan (type B1)

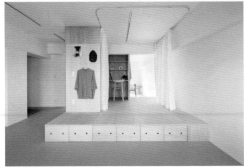

Floor plan (type B2)

2 4 6   9.84 ft
1   2   3 m

Sitting modestly in a street lined with ornate Victorian residences, this new home and architecture studio have been designed with reference to the previous Victorian house on the site: a weatherboard that was stripped of its Victorian features and transformed in 1956 to become an expression of modernist ideals.

SOUTH MELBOURNE BEACH HOUSE

Melbourne, Victoria, Australia
1,615 ft² (150 m²)
Design: Topology Studio
Stylist: Inside Story
Photography: Paul Hermes

This latest iteration similarly flaunts a beautiful tapestry of non-Victorian nuances that have been intricately woven to attribute a modern and inviting home. Spaces were opened up and a distinct identity was bestowed. The dining area and kitchen are placed at the front, facing the street and catching the morning light. A central courtyard separates and links spaces, effectively channeling light into the interior of the home. Views and connections from one room into another enhance the spatial generosity and provide an intricate flow throughout. Textures change across a consistent color, transforming the different areas through the day as the light shifts. Added to the mix, gardens and soft light create a feeling of relaxed informality. The compact design is a rigorous example of small-scale inner-city living, accommodating a family of four within a relatively small floor plan.

Designed as three elements: a timber box, masonry plinth, and sculptural form, the external envelope achieves simplicity and clarity through a refined material palette. Recycled brickwork and weathered timber cladding of Silvertop ash bring out the home's beachside setting, while also standing up to the elements.

"Small-scale, inner-city living for a family of four that pays homage to a 1950s expression of modernist ideals."

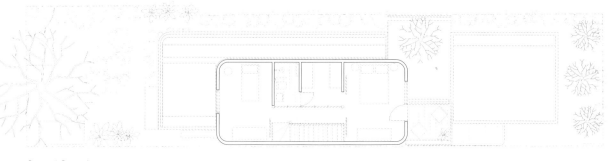

Second-floor plan

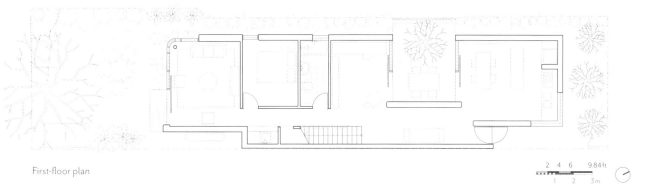

First-floor plan

2 4 6   9.84 ft
  1   2   3m

SURRY HILLS HOUSE

Sydney, Australia
969 ft² (90 m²)
Design: Benn & Penna Architects
Photography: Tom Ferguson

An introverted inner-city terrace in Sydney's eastern suburbs is given a face-lift with alterations and extensions to create a generously proportioned home flooded with natural light. The transformation also sought to form seamless connections between the different spaces in the house and the garden at the back. This resulted in an exaggerated linear form that playfully mocks the elongation of dwellings that is common sight in the narrow lots of Surry Hills.

A back wall was removed, extending the rear of the house so that the first-floor sprawls as a continuous indoor–outdoor space, shaping an open-plan kitchen and living room. Keeping up with the design concept, a long kitchen cabinet extends into the garden to house a barbecue, encouraging continuity in the flow of the space. The counter turns and meanders on, and drops a level to form a bench that faces the kitchen. A backdrop of white mosaic tiles reflects the northern light back into the garden and kitchen.

To that end, the design concept strategically selected materials and implemented modifications to amplify the presence of light inside the home. Pale timber flooring and white-painted walls convey a feeling of lightness in the interior and keep areas bright. Glass doors at entryways and a skylight in the living room also oblige the flow of natural light through the house.

In the middle of the house, a white, steel staircase with wooden treads accosts the open layout and ascends to a bathroom and a master bedroom with a private terrace. This light, understated interior was consciously crafted to complement and contrast the rich brickwork of neighboring residences in the Surry Hills suburbs. An enchanting white swan on a terra cotta sea.

"A face-lift with alterations and extensions creates a generously proportioned home flooded with natural light."

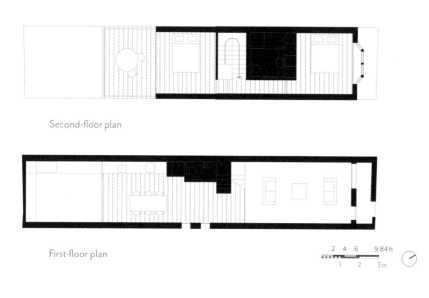

Second-floor plan

First-floor plan

2 4 6   9.84 ft
  1   2   3 m

Situated in what was once the BBC's iconic headquarters, this uber-stylish apartment is owned and designed by Sophie Ashby, and it reflects both her and her fashion designer husband Charlie's personal styles while paying homage to the building's endearing midcentury modern architecture.

TELEVISION CENTRE

London, United Kingdom
600 ft² (55 m²)
Design: Studio Ashby
Photography: Alexander James
Styling: Olivia Gregory

Buying the apartment off the plan allowed Sophie to fastidiously design the interior around the building's small proportions and original features. Limited space encouraged the tight curation and selection of versatile pieces. Of those, integrated storage and dual-purpose furniture took precedence. A sofa bed, furniture with wheels, and a bench on one side of the dining table allow for more space when the kitchen is in use. Intelligent cupboard doors that tag-team the ensemble conceal coats and the laundry to give the illusion of roominess.

Geometric bathroom tiles, a restored beamed ceiling, stylish Crittall windows, and African-inspired fabrics give the apartment a bold and dynamic feel. A photograph by Lakin Ogunbanwo takes center stage in the living room and highlights the bright ocher used on the bedroom walls. In the kitchen, a terrazzo countertop reflects the building's original floors. These striking design tendencies bring character, atmosphere, and feeling to this home.

"Limited space encouraged tight curation and a selection of versatile pieces."

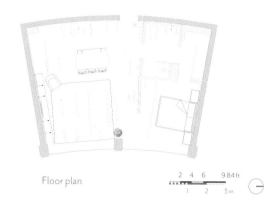

Floor plan

2 4 6   9.84 ft
1 2   3m

THORNBURY HOUSE

Melbourne, Victoria, Australia
1,894 ft² (176 m²)
Design: BENT Architecture
Photography: Tatjana Plitt

This award-winning house is a low-cost, compact family home set within a quiet inner suburb. The home's novel design is narrated through scale, materiality, and form, in both its overall expression and detailing. Thornbury House is a double-story residence in what appears to be a single-story dwelling, being a creative response to a compact footprint within the context of typically larger Australian suburban dwellings. The roof was stretched and pulled to accommodate an upper level, resulting in a playful sculptural form that is both referential to and divergent from the pitched roofs typical of the area.

Utilizing traditional construction techniques and cost-effective building materials, a highly considered architectural project is delivered within tight budget constraints. A courtyard and the generous use of windows allow spaces to feel expansive despite their modest size.

Living spaces face north and feature large windows, as well as sliding doors that open to both the rear yard and courtyard. This saturates these prime areas with light and traces a fluid connection between the inside and the lively outdoors. The captivating external views proffered are integral to the internal experience of each space and build a strong relationship between internal and external spaces.

The living area's ceiling is articulated in double-height, courtesy of the pitched roof, creating an alternative volume and a liberating shift in the scale of the space. Details such as full-height hardwood architraves, polished concrete slabs and plywood joinery weave textural richness and tailor a warm interior that invites time spent together, making the Thornbury House a home where the heart truly is.

> "A low-cost, compact design firmly embedded in scale, materiality, and form of context."

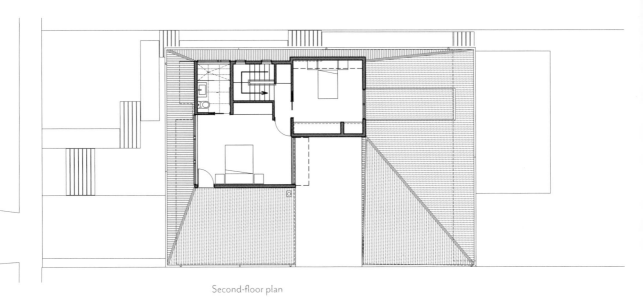

Second-floor plan

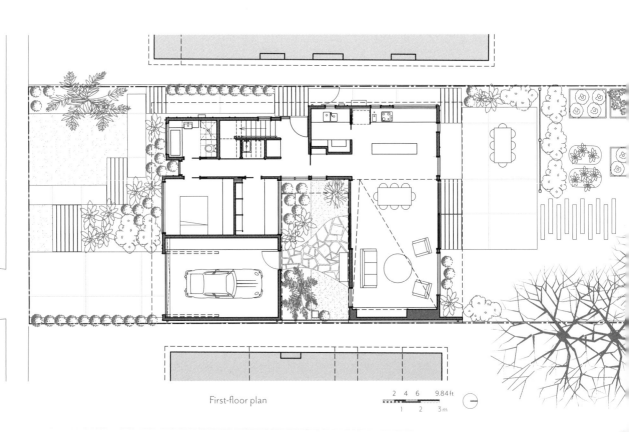

First-floor plan

2 4 6   9.84 ft
1   2   3 m

It sounds a little contradictory to build a tiny house for a tall guy but it turns out that 377 square feet (35 square meters) is enough space to create a dwelling that feels spacious and lofty. The owner sought a design that deliberately uses minimal space. By doing so, he would be able to achieve a small footprint and also have to consciously inhabit his home—filling it carefully by doing away with unnecessary items. The result: a clean, contemporary, and minimalistic way of living.

TINY HOUSE FOR A TALL GUY

Amsterdam, The Netherlands
377 ft² (35 m²)
Design: Julius Taminiau Architects
Photography: Norbert Wunderling

Quality over quantity was the driving concept for this design. The architect took a minimalistic approach, simplifying the design as much as possible to create a harmonious space that is bright, spacious and which includes plenty of storage. Everything was designed made-to-measure in 3D CAD and unnecessary partnerships (such as contractors) were eliminated. By by-passing a middleman contractor, materials could be ordered directly from suppliers and the building process could be better controlled, resulting in a more accurate design execution.

The unit is conceived as a single, open space, save for *one* dividing wall that conceals the laundry room and bathroom. The kitchen reiterates this open continuity by masking kitchen appliances within cabinetry. Woodwork is kept to the same tone so that the eye glides over the space as a whole without any stark demarcation of individual areas. The bedroom is portioned off from the living area with storage cabinets that feature a slated hollow. This design maintains privacy yet still lets light through. Neutral and natural materials allow for the innovative emphasis of the interior, highlighting its simplicity and pleasant austerity.

"Deliberate and minimalistic design that calls for a more conscious way of living."

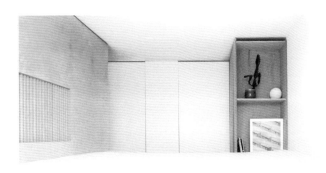

The designers maximized every last inch of this basic 1970s one-bedroom apartment to explore a central question: how do you fit a big house into a small unit? They declare that the trick to designing a home with a small footprint is knowing where it pays to be generous.

TYPE STREET APARTMENT

Melbourne, Victoria, Australia
377 ft² (35 m²)
Design: Tsai Design
Photography: Tess Kelly

Working within the constraints of the original floor plan, they poured their energy (and a modest budget) into floor-to-ceiling, multifunctional cabinetry and wall systems. This allowed abundant but concealed storage in every room—a feature often lacking in apartment living. The biggest kitchen possible was a must, and where there was once just a sink, there is now a roomy kitchen with ample bench space and concealed storage.

In the daytime, the kitchen borrows light streaming in from the bathroom window. It also offers mood-lifting peeks of the bathroom's garden wall, so kitchen chores are accompanied with revived energy. When the facilities are needed, a privacy-film-glass can be activated at the flick of a switch.

Several key design solutions create the illusion of space in an apartment that has standard-height ceilings. Mirrored cabinetry and skirting make the living room feel bigger; a fold-up desk in the office nook allows residents to pack work away at night; a retractable clothesline makes maximum use of the bathroom; and concealed air conditioning in the bedroom prevents ugly views of utility components. At just 377 square feet (35 square meters), Type Street Apartment is a small but undoubtedly impactful design. It is a space for entertaining, a home office, and a place of rest, all in one.

"The trick to designing small footprint homes is knowing where it pays to be generous."

First-floor plan

2 4 6   9.84 ft
1   2   3 m

UNYOKED

New South Wales & Victoria, Australia
151 ft² (14 m²)
Design: Fresh Prince
Photography: Sammy Hawker

Unyoked is a new travel concept of small cabins promising one-of-a-kind holiday experiences in Australia's bush. The inspiration for the venture materialized out of the urge to remedy the over-stimulation of everyday Western life.

Unyoked aims to redefine how people spend their leisure time by encouraging holidaymakers to escape urban density and give in to uninterrupted time in nature. In other words, provide "an ancient remedy for modern problems."

The architecturally designed cabins call out to a yearning for solitude and disconnection from the speed of modern life. Off-grid, simple, sustainable, and small were the main aspects underpinning the design of each dwelling. Intended to tread as lightly as possible on the landscape, each one has a minimal environmental footprint and incorporates solar power, reclaimed materials (such as re-purposed timber and windows), and a variety of outdoor amenities such as picnic tables, gas stoves, and fire pits. The special Yogie and Miguel cabins even make room for a pet friend to join the adventure.

Usually bordering forests, nestled in valleys, or planted in the mountains, each dwelling feels completely remote but is still accessible by car. Each location has been carefully considered and is completely removed from noise pollution and man-made distractions, allowing occupants to unplug, recharge, and practice contentment with less. And perhaps the experience will engender a love for living little.

"Inspired by an urge to remedy the over-stimulation of everyday Western life and redefine how we spend our leisure time."

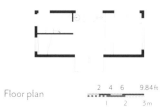

Floor plan

2 4 6   9.84 ft
1   2   3 m

URBAN COCOON

Paris, France
291 ft² (27 m²)
Design: Nathalie Eldan Architecture
Photography: David Foessel

Residing in an old cotton factory in Paris' lively rue de Charonne, Urban Cocoon is a reconfigured single-room duplex boasting an array of stylish but highly functional utilities.

Sleep, relaxation, and privacy are at the forefront of this design concept. Highlighting the sleeping area as the most important function, the bed is elevated on a platform with sliding wooden screens. The sleeping platform thus achieves a permanent presence within the room, giving preference to moments of downtime. It also helps to distinguish between the day and night areas.

Residents can manipulate the sliding screens into various configurations to provide complete privacy or absolute openness as so desired. When drawn shut, activities like reading, watching a movie, or having a nap turn the space into a quintessential urban cocoon. When the space within is lit, it transforms into an elegant and subtle lightbox that engages with the room *light*-heartedly.

At the heart of the design are two birch installations. In the day section of the room, an extra-large floor-to-ceiling unit works as an active wall, masking living essentials and appliances. It also frames a sink and a small counter for food preparation. The second unit at the base of the metal staircase acts as a connecting flight of stairs to the first floor and absorbs the water tank while simultaneously providing storage for shoes, coats, and suitcases.

"A reconfigured single-room duplex boasting an array of stylish but highly functional utilities tailored to daytime and night-time activities."

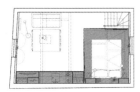

Second-floor plan

First-floor plan

2 4 6 9.84 ft
1 2 3 m

INDEX

INDEX

INDEX

Published in Australia in 2020 by
The Images Publishing Group Pty Ltd
ABN 89 059 734 431

Offices

Melbourne
6 Bastow Place
Mulgrave, Victoria 3170
Australia
Tel: +61 3 9561 5544

New York
6 West 18th Street 4B
New York, NY 10011
United States
Tel: +1 212 645 1111

Shanghai
6F, Building C, 838 Guangji Road
Hongkou District, Shanghai 200434 China
Tel: +86 021 31260822

books@imagespublishing.com
www.imagespublishing.com

Copyright © The Images Publishing Group Pty Ltd 2020
The Images Publishing Group Reference Number: 1545

All diagrams and plans are supplied by the participants, and photography is attributed throughout the book, with the following exceptions: page 2: Asier Rua (Miel Arquitectos, Piso Pereiv44); page 6: Paul Hermes (Topology Studio, South Melbourne Beach House); page 220: David Foessel (Nathalie Eldan Architecture, Urban Cocoon); endpapers: Pascal Otlinghaus (Glenn Medioni Agency, Buttes Chaumont)

A catalogue record for this
book is available from the
National Library of Australia

Title: Living Little: Simplicity and style in small spaces // text by Hannah Jenkins
ISBN: 9781864708608

This title was commissioned in IMAGES' Melbourne office and produced as follows: *Editorial coordination* Chandranie, *Art direction/production* Nicole Boehringer, *Senior editorial* Georgia (Gina) Tsarouhas, *Thanks also to* Jeanette Wall

Printed and bound in China by Artron Art Group on 140gsm Da Dong FSC® woodfree paper

IMAGES has included on its website a page for special notices in relation to this and its other publications. Please visit www.imagespublishing.com